HOW DOES IT KNOW

What Your Phone Knows About You

BRANDON GAUNCE

How Does It Know?

ISBN: 979-8-9961279-2-4

Cover design by Brandon Gaunce

Published by BDG Publishing

Printed in the United States of America

Contents

How Does It Know? 1

How Does It Know What I Want? 3

How Does It Know What Matters To Me? 12

How Does It Know What I'm Feeling? 22

How Does It Know When I Need To Hear It? 34

How Does It Know Before I Do? 47

How Does It Know What I'll See Next? 59

How Does It Know Who I Know? 71

Why Do I Keep Picking It Up? 80

Why Was I Listening? 84

Does It Know? 89

Discernment 98

It Knows Because You Told It 100

A Final Thought 102

How Does It Know?

At some point, almost all of us ask this question.

How does it know?

How many times have you thought about wanting something, only to see that exact thing appear in your feed? Or maybe you were going through something, in a relationship or at work, a rough patch, a hard week, something you hadn't told anyone, but somehow your feed was full of content that already knew. Was it a song, a video, or a message that showed up at the exact moment you needed it, like it was sitting there waiting on you?

That quiet little suspicion that something out there is paying attention. That it knows you a little too well. That it knew what you wanted before you did.

The easiest explanation, the one you probably reach for first, is that your phone is listening. And honestly, that's not a crazy thought. You know these devices collect information. You know companies are paying attention. You know the technology gets more sophisticated every year. When something shows up at exactly the right moment, it really does feel like someone is looking over your shoulder.

But that explanation doesn't cover everything.

What about the things you never said out loud? What about the stuff you only thought about? What about the feelings you never shared with anyone, let alone an app?

That's where it gets interesting.

This book started with that question. Not because I had all the answers, but because I kept noticing how many people were asking it. People like you. Smart, skeptical, not looking for a conspiracy, just an explanation.

Because something is happening. What you're noticing is real. The question is what's behind it.

We're going to get into all of it. The algorithms, the data, the psychology, the business models, the moments that feel impossible and the ones that turn out to have a straightforward explanation. Some of what you'll read here will make total sense. Some of it will probably make you look at your phone a little differently.

But let's start where you probably did.

How Does It Know What I Want?

You didn't go looking for it.

That's the weird part.

You weren't shopping. You weren't searching. You didn't type anything, click anything, or even say anything out loud. You just kind of thought about it. Maybe mentioned it to someone. Maybe you just saw it briefly while you were doing something else entirely.

And then there it was.

An ad. Right in your feed. The exact thing you'd been thinking about.

And you thought, okay, that's bizarre.

You probably let it go the first time. Weird coincidence, whatever. But then it happens again and then again. At some point you stop calling it a coincidence and start wondering if something out there is actually paying attention to you.

The answer is, Yes, it is.

Just not in the way you probably think.

Teeth Whitening

Let's start small.

You're brushing your teeth one morning, catch yourself in the mirror, and think, when did my teeth get so stained? You don't say it out loud. You don't search for anything. You just have that quiet little moment of self-consciousness and move on with your day.

Unexpectedly, whitening strips show up in your feed.

And you think, okay, WTH?

It wasn't the creepy version. Nobody was watching you look in the mirror. No one heard you think it. What actually happened is a lot less creepy and truthfully, sort of more interesting.

The system already had a pretty good idea you'd want whiter teeth.

Not you specifically. But a version of you. Built from months, maybe years of data. Your age range, your location, what you buy, what you browse, what kind of content you slow down for. People with similar profiles tend to start thinking about their appearance around certain times of year. Maybe you'd been lingering on certain content lately without realizing it. Maybe something in your pattern changed just enough to nudge the algorithm toward that exact item. The silent system that decides what you see.

You didn't search for whiter teeth. You were predicted into it.

Being predicted is completely different from being watched. Once you get your head around that, a lot of this starts to make a lot more sense.

The Ad That Followed You

What about the shoes?

You looked at a pair of shoes on a website. You didn't buy them; you just closed the window and moved on with your life. Then those shoes just started following you around the internet. News sites. Social media. Random apps that have nothing to do with shopping.

For days.

This one actually has a name. It's called retargeting. When you visit a website, tiny bits of code, cookies, tracking pixels, little invisible things, they notice you were there and pass that information along to advertising networks. Those networks then show you ads for that product on basically any site that's part of the same system.

The shoe company isn't following you personally. They've just paid to remind everyone who visited their site without buying that, Hey, those shoes are still there.

It feels personal. It is personal. But it's also just a machine doing exactly what it was trained to do.

Following You Around The Internet

The internet you're using isn't everyone's internet.

It's your internet. A version of it that's been shaped around everything you've ever done online.

Every site you visit. Every link you click. Every search you make. Every video you watch and every video you skip ten seconds into. Every product you look at. Every article you abandon halfway through. All of it gets recorded, sorted, and fed into systems that are trying to figure out who you are and what you want.

They're not just looking at what you do. They're looking at how you do it.

How long you pause on something before scrolling past. What time of day you're most active. What kind of content makes you stop. What makes you keep going. How fast you scroll. The pattern of it.

None of that feels like information you're giving away. But you are. Every single day.

The Data Trail

You probably don't think about this part.

You're not just being tracked on one platform. You're being tracked across all of them. Across devices. Over time.

Something you searched on your laptop last month can still influence what you see on your phone today. A product you looked at once and never thought about again is sitting in a file somewhere with your name on it. Not your name exactly, but something that points straight to you.

Your location history. Your purchase history. Your browsing history. The apps on your phone. The loyalty cards linked to your email. The wifi networks you connect to.

It adds up to a picture. A pretty detailed one, and you built it yourself just by living your life.

The Business Of Attention

None of this exists because someone is out to get you.

It exists because there's an enormous amount of money in knowing what people want.

The more precisely a platform can predict what you're interested in, the more it can charge someone else for access to your attention. Advertisers don't want to show you random stuff. They want to show you the right stuff at the right time. That's worth a lot of money to them.

So the platforms get very good at understanding you. Not because they care about you, but because your attention is worth something and they want to sell it.

You're not the customer. You're the merchandise.

You've probably heard that before. But it's one of those things that's easy to accept but harder to actually believe. Every time you open an app for free, something is happening in the background. Your behavior is being studied, packaged, and sold to people who want to reach you.

That's the deal. You just never read the terms.

Is My Phone Listening?

At some point the experiences get strange enough that people reach for the simplest explanation.

Your phone is listening.

And frankly? It makes sense as a theory. You know your phone has a microphone. You know companies collect more than they admit. When an ad shows up for something you talked about but never searched, what else are you supposed to think?

Research actually shows something different, though. The kind of surveillance most people imagine is that your phone is constantly recording conversations, listening for keywords, triggering ads in real time, that's not what's happening. Not because it's impossible. Because it's not necessary.

They don't need to listen to you.

They already know enough.

There's data about your behavior, your patterns, your history, the people around you, the places you go. It's detailed enough to make predictions that feel just as eerie as if someone had been listening the whole time.

Your phone doesn't need to hear you say you want a new coffee maker. It already knows you're probably thinking about one right now.

Prediction, Not Surveillance

This is the part that should change how you see all of it.

Surveillance means someone is watching. Prediction means a system is guessing. The difference between those two is greater than it sounds.

Surveillance would mean someone heard you mention a coffee maker and placed an ad. Prediction means a system noticed that people with your profile tend to replace small appliances around this time of year, that you've been spending more time on home related content lately, that your patterns point to a certain kind of change and decided a coffee maker ad was worth showing you.

Nobody listened. A pattern was recognized.

To you, it feels exactly the same, either way. That's what makes it so hard to wrap your head around and easy to mistake for something more sinister than it actually is.

Why Some Ads Feel Like Mind-Reading

And yet.

Some of it still doesn't add up.

You think about something without searching for it, without saying it, without doing anything that obviously connects, but it shows up anyway. Those are the ones that really get under your skin.

Some of those moments are just coincidence. You remember the ones that relate and forget the hundreds of ads that had nothing to do with anything. The ones that connect feel like magic. The rest you don't even notice.

But some of it is influences you can't see. Someone in your house searched for something on the same wifi network. A friend mentioned something in a group chat on a platform with data sharing agreements you didn't know existed. A store credit card linked to your email quietly connected an in-store purchase to your online profile.

The systems talk to each other more than you realize.

In reality, some of it just hasn't been fully explained yet. Not because your phone is listening. But because the data is extensive enough, and the predictions are good enough, that the line between knowing and guessing gets very thin.

It's not mind reading.

But it's not all coincidence either.

How Does It Know What Matters To Me?

You ever get one of those messages that stops you mid-scroll?

Not because it was flashy or loud. Just because it said exactly the right thing at exactly the right moment. Something that felt less like content and more like someone had been reading your mind.

Maybe it was a quote. Maybe it was a video. Maybe it was one of those posts that's technically written for everyone but somehow felt like it was written for you specifically. Like whoever made it knew what you were going through at that moment.

You might have saved it, shared it, or just watched it a second longer than everything else.

That feeling of being observed by something that shouldn't be able to see you is what this section is about.

A lot of what shows up in your feed isn't personal at all. It just feels that way. Understanding why it feels that way turns out to be just as interesting as understanding the technology behind it.

It's not just about what the algorithm knows about you. It's about how your brain is wired to find meaning. Those two things together are a pretty powerful combination.

This Message Is For You

There's a reason certain content stops you cold.

It's not always because it's accurate, it's because it's open enough to feel accurate. A post that says you've been carrying a lot lately, and people keep underestimating you. It isn't describing you specifically. It's describing a feeling that a huge number of people have at any given moment. Stress. Self-doubt. The sense that you're doing more than anyone notices.

You feel that way sometimes. A lot of people feel that way right now.

So when that message appears in your feed it doesn't feel generic. It feels targeted. It feels like someone reached through the screen and said, yeah, I see you.

That's not surveillance. That's just really good writing aimed at a really universal feeling.

But the algorithm does its part too. It learned that you slow down for this kind of content. That you engage with it. That it keeps you on the app a little longer than a funny video or a news headline would. So it shows you more of it. The more it shows you the more it seems to understand you, and the more it seems to understand you, the more you engage.

It becomes a loop pretty quickly.

Take What Resonates

It's worth knowing how you actually process information.

You take what fits and leave what doesn't. It's not a flaw. It's just how you're wired. When something matches your experience you notice it and hold onto it. When it doesn't match you move past it and mostly forget it was ever there.

This is why horoscopes work on people who believe in them. Not because they're accurate, but because they're written broadly enough that something almost always relates. You read your horoscope and the part that fits your life right now jumps out. The parts that don't fit just kind of disappear.

Your feed works the same way. You're shown a huge volume of content every day. Some of it connects. Most of it doesn't. But the stuff that connects feels significant. It feels chosen. It feels like more than coincidence.

So you remember it that way.

The Search For Meaning

People have always looked for signs.

That's not a criticism. It's just true. You've always needed things to mean something. You look for patterns. You connect dots. You take the chaos of everyday life and try to find some kind of order in it.

When life gets uncertain, when something ends, when something hurts, when you're trying to figure out what comes next, that search for meaning gets stronger. You want to know that things happen for a reason. You want reassurance. You want someone or something to tell you you're going to be okay.

Social media figured out a long time ago that there's a massive appetite for that.

And it delivers.

Astrology, Psychics, Tarot Readings, Twin Flames

If you've ever gone through a hard breakup, a major life change, or just a long stretch of uncertainty, you've probably encountered this corner of social media.

Astrology, Psychics, Tarot readings, Twin flame content. All of it sitting right there in your feed, sometimes before you even went looking for it.

And some of it connects. Hard.

The astrology post that captures something you've been feeling but couldn't name. The psychic who seems to be describing your exact situation. The tarot reader who lays out a dynamic so specifically that you screenshot it and send it to three people. The twin flame video that puts words to something you hadn't admitted to yourself yet.

So what's actually happening?

These formats are specifically designed to feel personal without being personal. A tarot reader filming a general reading for their entire audience uses language that's intentionally open. They talk about someone pulling away, about hidden feelings, about a connection that won't quite let go. Those themes apply to so many people at once that the odds of them landing for someone watching are extremely high.

It's not a trick exactly. A lot of the people making that content genuinely believe in what they're doing. But the reason it feels like they're reading your situation isn't because they are. It's because they're describing human experiences that are almost universal, and your brain is doing the rest of the work.

Then the algorithm kicks in.

Once you slow down for one of those videos, once you watch it to the end or save it or click on the creator's profile, the system notices. It knows what kept you there, and it starts filling your feed with more of it. More astrology. More readings. More twin flame content. More content aimed at exactly the emotional place you're in.

It's not that the algorithm understands your heartbreak. It just knows you'll watch.

Religious Messages, Manifestation Content, Relationship Advice

The same thing happens across all of it.

A bible verse that appears at exactly the moment you needed to hear it. A manifestation video that speaks directly to something you've been working through. A relationship advice post that describes your situation so accurately it gives you chills.

None of it is coincidence. None of it is mind reading either.

It's a combination of content designed to feel universal and an algorithm that's very good at learning what keeps you engaged. The more you interact with a certain type of content the more of it you see. The more of it you see, the more chances there are for something to connect, and when something connects it feels like so much more than an algorithm doing its job.

It feels like the universe talking.

Why Generic Messages Feel Personal

There's a name for this. It's called the Barnum effect.

P.T. Barnum, the circus guy, supposedly said there's a sucker born every minute. Whether he actually said it or not, the effect named after him is real, and it applies to you too, not just the suckers.

The Barnum effect is the tendency to accept vague, general statements as uniquely accurate descriptions of yourself. Personality tests use it. Horoscopes use it. It's how a psychic convinces a room full of strangers that every word is meant for them. Huge amounts of social media content use it whether it's intentional or not.

When something feels written just for you there's a good chance it was written for everyone. And your brain made it personal.

The Feeling Of Being Seen

But here's the part that actually matters.

Even when you understand all of this, even when you know about the Barnum effect and the algorithm and the content designed to feel personal, the feeling doesn't completely go away.

Because the feeling of being seen is one of the most powerful human experiences there is. You want it. You need it. And in a world where so many people feel increasingly disconnected, finding it anywhere, even in a tarot video made for ten million strangers, does something real.

That much is real.

The algorithm didn't understand you. But for a second it felt like something did, and sometimes that's enough to make you stop scrolling.

How Does It Know What I'm Feeling?

Your feed doesn't always feel the same.

You've probably noticed that without ever really thinking about it. Some days you open an app and everything feels light. Funny videos. Good news. Things that make you smile without trying. Other days it feels heavier. More emotional. Like the whole thing shifted overnight without warning.

You didn't change the settings. You didn't ask for anything different.

But the feed knew anyway.

Or at least it seemed to.

That's what this section is about. Not just what the algorithm shows you but how it seems to track something underneath the surface. Something that doesn't show up in a search bar or a purchase history.

So, How does it know what you're feeling?

The Feed Feels Different

The platforms know something you probably don't.

Your behavior changes when your mood changes. Not in obvious ways. Not in ways you'd necessarily notice yourself. But the data does.

When you're in a good place you scroll differently. You engage differently. You click on different things, watch different content, move through the app at a different pace. When you're anxious or sad or stressed those patterns shift. You slow down on certain things. You skip past others. You linger on content that matches where you are emotionally even if you're not consciously choosing it.

The algorithm isn't reading your emotions; it's reading your behavior. But your behavior is a pretty accurate reflection of your emotions whether you realize it or not.

So the feed shifts. Not because it understands you, but because it noticed what you're doing and adjusted accordingly.

When You're Having A Bad Day

You don't have to tell it.

That's the part that catches people off guard. You don't post about it. You don't search for anything that would give it away. You just open the app because you need somewhere to put your attention for a few minutes and suddenly the content feels different. More emotional. More validating. More of the stuff that fits exactly how you feel right now.

It's not magic, just pattern recognition running at a scale you can't really picture.

The system has seen millions of people behave the way you're behaving right now. It knows what types of content those people engaged with. It knows what kept them on the app when they were in the same kind of mood, and it's giving you that content too.

Not because it cares how you're doing. Because keeping you on the app is the whole point.

It Knows Your Hours

Your phone knows your hours better than you do. It knows the moment you wake and reach for it. It knows your mid-afternoon slump. It knows you scroll late at night.

Not because anyone wrote it down, but because you do the same things at the same times, and patterns are the easiest thing in the world to spot. So it learns your windows. The hours you're bored. The hours you're soft.

It doesn't need to know why you're up at 2 a.m. It just needs to know that you are.

Hope

When you're looking for hope, you behave in a very specific way online.

You slow down for comeback stories. For content about things working out. For videos about people who went through something hard and came out the other side. You watch longer. You save more. You share more.

The algorithm sees all of that. It sees the saves and the shares and the extra seconds spent watching. It learns that you respond to hopeful content right now, and it decides to give you more.

So it does.

The feed starts to feel almost encouraging. Like it's rooting for you. Like it somehow knows you needed a reason to believe things are going to be okay.

It doesn't know you. But it figured you out anyway.

What's worth paying attention to is, how good that feels. A feed that seems to believe in you is hard to put down. And the app knows that too.

Fear

Fear works differently.

Content that triggers anxiety or worry tends to get a lot of engagement. Not because you enjoy being scared but because fear is hard to look away from. You're wired that way. Threat detection is one of the oldest things your brain does, and it hasn't adjusted to something like a social media feed.

So when you're already anxious the algorithm often makes it worse without meaning to. It's not trying to scare you. It's just learned that this kind of content keeps anxious people engaged. And keeping you there is all it's trying to do. Fear content isn't a side effect. It's a known category. It hooks people, it holds them, and it reliably makes money. The algorithm didn't stumble onto this. It learned it.

The result is that a bad day can spiral into a very bad evening pretty quickly if you're not paying attention to what's happening.

Loneliness

Loneliness is one of the most common human experiences and one of the least talked about ones.

You don't usually post about feeling lonely. You don't search for it. But the behavior that comes with it has a signature. More time on the app. Slower scrolling. More engagement with content about connection, relationships, belonging. More time spent watching videos of people who feel like they get it.

The algorithm recognizes that signature. Maybe not perfectly. Maybe not every time. But often enough that your feed starts filling with content that speaks to that feeling exactly.

Connection content. Community content. Videos that feel like company.

For a lot of people that's genuinely comforting. Until it isn't. Until you realize you've been on your phone for two hours and the loneliness is still there and maybe actually worse than when you started.

Because the app gave you the feeling of connection without any of the things that actually make a connection work. No one heard you. No one responded. Nothing changed. You just watched other people talk about life until you finally put the phone down.

Heartbreak

Heartbreak might be the clearest example of all of this.

Because heartbreak changes everything about how you use your phone. You check it more. You scroll longer. You look at things you probably shouldn't look at. You're drawn to content about love and loss and starting over and whether things can be fixed or whether you should let them go.

All of that behavior is data.

And the algorithm takes that data and fills your world with more of the same. More relationship content. More healing content. More of the tarot readers and the astrology posts and the anonymous quotes about missing someone.

It's not trying to help you heal. It's trying to keep you scrolling. Those two things just happen to overlap.

Validation

This one's easy to miss, because it feels so good when it happens.

Validation content, stuff that tells you you're right, you're not crazy, you deserve better, the other person was the problem, is some of the most engaging content on the internet.

When you're hurting, when you're angry, when you're questioning yourself, something that tells you you're okay is almost impossible to scroll past. It feels like relief. It feels like someone finally gets it.

The algorithm learns that fast. It sees you engaging with that kind of content and it brings you more of it. More of, you deserve better content. More of, they never appreciated you. More of, your feelings are valid.

After a while your entire feed is one long echo of your own emotions reflected back at you.

Louder each time.

The Emotional Mirror

That's actually a pretty good way to think about what the feed becomes when this is all running at full speed.

A mirror.

Not a window into the world. A reflection of wherever you are emotionally right now. Amplified and optimized to keep you looking.

The problem with mirrors is that they don't push back. They don't offer a different perspective. They don't tell you something you don't already think or feel. They just show you yourself, over and over, until that reflection feels like the whole picture.

When Content Becomes Company

For a lot of people, their feed fills a void.

When you're lonely, when you're going through something, when the people in your life aren't available or don't quite get it, your phone is always there. The content is always there. Some of it genuinely helps. A video that makes you laugh when you needed to laugh. A story that makes you feel less alone in something you thought only you went through.

That's real. That matters.

But there's a difference between content that helps you feel better and content that keeps you feeling bad enough to keep scrolling. The algorithm doesn't know which one you need. It only knows which one keeps you on the app.

Does The Feed Understand Emotion?

Not really. Not the way another person would.

It doesn't feel anything. It doesn't care how your day went. It has no idea what you're actually going through.

What it has is data. Enormous amounts of it, and that data is detailed enough that the feed can behave as if it understands you, even when it fundamentally doesn't.

That gap between behaving like it understands and actually understanding is worth keeping in mind every time the feed feels a little too personal.

It's not reading your heart.

It's reading your behavior.

And those two things are closer together than you'd like to admit.

How Does It Know When I Need To Hear It?

Some things you just can't explain away.

You're driving somewhere, thinking about someone you haven't spoken to in years, and a song comes on that the two of you used to listen to together. You're dealing with something heavy, trying to figure out what to do, and you pick up your phone and the first thing you see is a quote that speaks directly to exactly what you're thinking about. You're having one of the worst weeks you've had in a long time and a video finds you that makes you feel like someone out there gets it.

You think, there is no way that's a coincidence.

Maybe it isn't.

Or maybe the answer is somewhere in between what we want it to be and what it actually is. Which happens to be one of the more interesting places to look.

That Can't Be A Coincidence

Here's the thing about coincidences.

You're terrible at calculating them.

You're not wired to accurately assess probability. You're wired to notice patterns. To find meaning. To connect things that happen close together in time and assume they must be connected in some deeper way too.

That's not a flaw exactly. For most of human history that instinct has kept us alive. Noticing a pattern and reacting to it fast was far more useful than standing around trying to work out the odds.

But it also means you see connections that aren't there. You remember the moments that felt significant and forget the thousands of ordinary moments around them. And when something connects at exactly the right time, you feel it in a way that's hard to rationalize away even when you know you probably should.

The Song

Music is one of the most powerful triggers you have.

A song doesn't just bring back a memory. It brings back the feeling connected with that memory. The specific emotional texture of a moment you lived years ago. The person you were then. The thing you were feeling. All of it arrives with the first few notes in a way that almost nothing else can replicate.

So when a song shows up at exactly the right moment it feels different than almost anything else can.

But here's what's worth thinking about. Streaming platforms and algorithm driven radio have an enormous amount of data about your listening history. They know what you listened to during certain periods of your life. They know what you return to when your listening patterns shift. They know that certain songs in your history are associated with certain emotional states based on when you played them, how often and what else you were listening to around the same time.

They're not reading your memories. But they're not guessing blindly either.

The Quote

A perfectly timed quote feels like a message.

Almost like something or someone put it there specifically for you to find right now. The feeling is real, even when the explanation is pretty straightforward.

Quotes are designed to be universal. The best ones describe human experiences in ways that are specific enough to feel personal but broad enough to apply to almost anyone going through almost anything. Grief. Love. Uncertainty. The feeling that something is ending or beginning or both at the same time.

When you're in the middle of something emotionally, your brain is primed to find relevance everywhere. You're scanning for meaning. You're looking for something that fits, and when something fits it fits completely. It doesn't feel like you found a quote. It feels like the quote found you.

The algorithm helped. It knew you were in a certain emotional place based on your behavior and it surfaced content that tends to resonate with people in that place. But your brain did most of the work.

The Video

Videos land harder than almost anything else.

A real person on a screen talking directly into the camera about something they've been through. Something that sounds like your situation. The specific details might be different but the feeling is exactly the same, and they're looking right at you.

That kind of content is engineered, sometimes intentionally, sometimes just instinctively by creators who've learned what works, to create the feeling of a direct personal connection. The casual setting. The unpolished delivery. The way they say things like "you know that feeling when..." and your answer is, "Yes. I do know that feeling."

It's not fake. The person making it probably went through something real. But it's also not specifically about you. It just feels that way because the best version of that content is made to feel that way.

And the algorithm got it to you because it knew you were ready to receive it.

Perfect Timing

How much of perfect timing is the universe and how much of it is just math?

The platforms you use are pushing content at you constantly. Hundreds of pieces of content a day. Thousands over the course of a week. The odds that some of it is going to come across at exactly the right moment aren't actually that low when you think about the volume.

The algorithm isn't random. It's specifically trying to show you things that match where you are right now. So the timing isn't just luck. It's a system optimized to find the right moment and it has enough data about you to get pretty close, pretty often.

That doesn't make the feeling less real. But it does change what's behind it.

Looking For Meaning

When you're going through something, you look for signs.

That's just human. It's always been human. Long before algorithms and smartphones and social media feeds, people were finding meaning in the world around them. A bird at the window. A number that kept appearing. A song on the radio at exactly the right moment.

The impulse to find meaning in coincidence isn't something the internet created. It just gave that impulse a much bigger playing field.

Now instead of a handful of meaningful moments finding you in a day there are thousands of pieces of short form content moving through your field of vision. The chances of something feeling significant go way up, and the feeling when it happens is just as powerful as it ever was.

Pattern Recognition

Your brain is the best pattern recognition machine ever built.

It is so good at finding patterns that it finds them even when they aren't there. And that's by design. A brain that occasionally sees patterns that don't exist is much more useful for survival than a brain that misses patterns that do.

But it means you're not equipped to evaluate your own experience of coincidence very accurately.

You feel the pattern. You feel the meaning. You feel that something arrived at exactly the right moment, and that feeling is real, and it matters. But the story you tell yourself about why it happened is often wrong in the most interesting ways.

The Frequency Effect

Have you ever learned a new word and then started hearing it everywhere?

Or bought a car and then suddenly noticed that exact car on every road you drove on?

That's the frequency effect. Also called the Baader-Meinhof phenomenon.

It's not that the word or the car suddenly became more common. It's that your brain started flagging it. Once something enters your awareness your brain prioritizes it. You notice it where you wouldn't have noticed it before.

The same thing happens with meaningful content. Once you're going through something your brain starts looking for it everywhere. And the feed is delivering thousands of pieces of content. The combination means you're going to find what you're looking for whether it was put there intentionally or not.

Synchronicity

The experience of two unrelated things occurring together in a way that feels meaningful. Not caused by each other. Just connected in a way that seems like more than chance.

Carl Jung called it synchronicity.

He thought it pointed to something real about the nature of reality. A kind of meaningful coincidence that exists beyond simple cause and effect. A lot of people still feel that way, and genuinely that's not a conversation this book is going to try to resolve.

What's worth saying is this. The feeling of synchronicity, of something arriving at exactly the right moment, is one of the most moving experiences you can have. It can feel like proof of something larger. Like the world is paying attention.

Whether it is or not is a different question entirely.

What the algorithm didn't do is make that feeling less real. The moment still happened. You still felt it. Whatever caused it, you were moved by it. That part belongs entirely to you.

The Timing Problem

This is where it gets complicated.

Even when you account for all of it, the volume of content, the frequency effect, the pattern seeking brain, the algorithm tuned to whatever you're feeling, there are still moments that don't fully add up.

Moments where the timing is so specific, the content so precise, the feeling so undeniable that the straightforward explanation doesn't quite cover it.

Maybe there's more going on. Maybe the systems are more sophisticated than we fully understand yet. Maybe the data being collected is more detailed than most people realize. Maybe the connections between platforms and devices and behavioral signals are extensive enough to produce results that genuinely look like something else.

Or maybe some things just happen.

The candid answer is that not everything has been fully explained.

Maybe that's okay. Living with a little uncertainty about technology doesn't mean you're naive. It means you're paying attention to something the clean explanations don't fully cover.

Why Certain Messages Arrive At The Right Moment

So why does it happen?

The straightforward answer is, probably all of the above.

Sophisticated systems that know more about your emotional state than you might expect. A brain that's primed to find meaning and remember the moments that feel significant. An enormous volume of content increasing the odds that something will connect. Algorithms are specifically optimized to reach you when you're most receptive.

And maybe there is something else. Something that doesn't fit neatly into any of those categories.

The moments that feel like more than coincidence might be coincidence. They might be prediction. They might be pattern recognition running in both directions, the system learning your patterns and your brain finding patterns in the system.

Or they might be exactly what they feel like. More than coincidence.

That's the part nobody can fully answer yet.

And really that might be the most interesting part of all.

How Does It Know Before I Do?

The algorithm knew a version of you before you did.

Not the one that exists today. The future you. The version that's six months away from wanting something you haven't thought of yet. The one that's about to go through something, buy something, change something or need something.

That version of you already exists in the data.

And the system is already preparing for that.

This is the part that tends to make you the most uncomfortable. Not the targeted ads. Not the emotional mirroring. Not even the feeling that something is listening. It's the idea that a machine might understand where you're headed before you do. That your future, or at least a pretty good guess of it, is already sitting in a database somewhere being used to sell you things.

That's a strange thing to think about.

But it's worth understanding because it's truer than you might realize.

The You Before You

Think about your major shifts in your life.

The time you changed jobs. The relationship that started or ended. The move to a new city. The health kick that you actually stuck with for a while. The phase where you got really into something new.

None of those things happened overnight. They built up. There were weeks or months of small signals before anything became obvious. A gradual shift in what you were reading, watching, thinking about. A slow change in your patterns.

You probably didn't notice it happening. But the data did.

That's the version of you before you. The version of yourself that exists in your behavioral patterns before you've consciously acknowledged what's coming. The algorithm is very good at finding that version of you and figuring out what you're going to need.

People Like You

Think about data at scale.

You are not the first person to go through whatever you're going through right now. Not even close. Millions of people have gone through versions of it before you, and a lot of them were using the same apps, the same platforms, the same devices when it happened.

Which means their behavioral data exists, and it can be compared to yours.

This is one of the most powerful things these systems do. They don't just look at you in isolation. They look at everyone who has ever behaved the way you're behaving right now and ask what did those other people do next. What did they buy. What did they need. What kept them on the app. What did their life look like six months later.

Then they use that to predict you.

Not perfectly. But well enough to be useful. Well enough to be profitable. Well enough to feel like something that knows you a little too well.

Patterns Of Attention

What you pay attention to is one of the most revealing things about you.

Not just what you search for or what you buy. What you slow down for. What you hover over without clicking. What you watch halfway through and then back up and watch again. What you screenshot. What you read to the very end even when you hadn't planned to.

These patterns are incredibly specific to individuals. The way you scroll through content has a fingerprint. That fingerprint carries information about your state of mind, your current preoccupations, the things you're working through, whether consciously or not.

The system reads that fingerprint constantly, and it updates its understanding of you every time you interact with anything.

Creatures Of Habit

You're more predictable than you like to think.

That's not an insult. It's just true. You're a creature of habit in ways that go much deeper than your morning routine or the route you take to work. Your emotional cycles have patterns. Your spending has patterns. Your attention has patterns. The way you move through periods of change and stability follows patterns that, when you zoom out to millions of people, are remarkably consistent.

The platforms have seen enough of those patterns to know approximately where you are in yours.

When someone starts spending more time on fitness content after months of ignoring it, the system knows that pattern. It's seen it thousands of times. It knows what usually comes next. It knows what that person is likely to buy, engage with, and respond to over the next few weeks.

It doesn't know your story. But it knows the form of it.

How It Predicts You

The technical term for all of this is predictive analytics.

Which sounds very corporate and dry, but what it actually means is using past behavior to make educated guesses about future behavior. And the guesses have gotten very good.

Not because technology is magic, but because the data is enormous. When you have behavioral data on hundreds of millions of people over many years, patterns emerge that are detailed enough to make predictions that feel almost personal.

In 2012, Target famously figured out a teenager was pregnant before her father did. Not because they were spying on her, but because her purchasing patterns shifted in ways that matched other people who turned out to be pregnant. They sent her coupons for baby products. Her father was furious. The store wasn't being clever. It was just running the numbers.

That story made headlines because it felt like a violation. But it's the same system that shows you an ad for something you were thinking about. Just more consequential. The difference is scale. Target was predicting one thing about one person. These systems are predicting thousands of things about hundreds of millions of people, every day, in ways that almost never make headlines because they almost never feel like a violation. They just feel like a really good recommendation.

Why It Recommends What It Does

Under all of this is one piece of technology doing the heavy lifting. The part of the app whose only job is to decide what clip you see next, what video plays after that and what shows up the second you open it.

This is the part worth thinking about. These systems don't trust what you say. They trust what you do.

You might tell a survey you want to see more news and less junk. You might tell yourself you're going to spend less time on your phone tonight. The system has heard all of that before and it has watched what actually happens next. The clicks. The replays. The three a.m. scroll you didn't plan on, and it has learned that the gap between what people say they want and what they actually do is enormous.

So it stopped listening to the stated version of you and started watching the real one. Not the person you describe when someone asks. The person you are when you think no one's looking.

That's an uncomfortable thing to know about yourself. It's also why the predictions work.

Knowing Before You Know

When the algorithm gets ahead of you, it's disturbing in a specific way.

Content starts appearing about things you've barely begun to think about. A new city you're apparently thinking about moving to. A career shift that's been sitting in the back of your mind. A relationship dynamic you haven't completely admitted to yourself but have thought about.

This makes you stop and think, did I make that obvious somehow?

Probably not in any single obvious way. But in a hundred small ways, across dozens of interactions, over weeks or months, a pattern emerged, and the system caught it before you knew it yourself.

That isn't the machine reading your mind. It's the machine being very good at reading the signals your mind sends out without your consent.

Future Purchases

This is the most straightforward version of prediction and the one that's easiest to understand.

Everything has a replacement cycle. Appliances. Cars. Phones. Clothing. Even relationships with brand name products tend to follow patterns. The system knows when people like you tend to upgrade, replace, or switch. It knows what usually triggers those decisions and it starts showing you relevant content before you've consciously decided on anything.

So you're not being manipulated into buying something you don't need. You're being reached at the moment you're most likely to be open to it.

Which is either very convenient or slightly alarming depending on how you look at it.

Future Interests

Interests follow patterns too.

When someone gets into running, they tend to get into nutrition. When someone gets into meditation they tend to get into certain kinds of books. When someone goes through a breakup, they often develop a sudden interest in things they'd ignore if they were with someone.

The algorithm has seen all of these patterns so many times that it can often predict your next interest before you've discovered it yourself. Which is why your feed can sometimes feel like it's a few steps ahead of you. Introducing you to things before you knew you were looking for them.

Sometimes that feels like discovery. Sometimes it feels like being stalked.

Both might be.

Future Decisions

The most uncomfortable version of all of this is the idea that major decisions might be predictable too.

Not just what you'll buy or what show you'll watch next. But bigger things. Where you'll live. Who you'll be with. What you'll do for work. Whether you'll stay or go.

The research suggests that even these decisions leave tracks long before you make them. Someone who's about to upend their life starts moving through the world a little differently, and that shift shows up in the data before the decision ever does.

Which means somewhere in a database a prediction exists about a decision you haven't made yet.

That's worth thinking about.

How Predictable Are You?

More than we want to be, but less than the systems pretend.

The predictions are good. Genuinely impressive. But they're also wrong a lot. They work for crowds, not for you specifically. The system might know that thirty percent of people in your situation make a certain decision. It doesn't know which thirty percent.

You are not just your data. Your history is not your destiny. The pattern is not the person. There's always a part of you that hasn't happened yet and predicting it isn't the same as choosing it.

However the pattern is real, and it's being read constantly by systems that have a financial interest in knowing what you're going to do before you do it.

The question isn't whether they can predict you.

It's whether knowing that changes anything.

How Does It Know What I'll See Next?

Two people can open the exact same app at the exact same moment and see completely different worlds.

One of them sees political news. Outrage. Something to be angry about. The other sees cooking videos, home renovation content and a dog doing something silly. Another person sees fitness motivation, supplement ads and before and after transformations. Yet, another person sees spiritual content, relationship advice, and videos about healing.

Same app. Same moment. Completely different realities.

No one chooses that. Not consciously anyway. It just happens. Gradually, quietly, formed by a thousand small interactions that added up to a feed that feels completely natural and completely personal even though it was never actually built for you. It was built by you, one tap at a time.

That's what this section is about. Not just what you see but who decided you would see it and whether anyone's really in control of it at all.

The Feed You Never Built

You didn't build your feed.

That's worth saying, because it doesn't feel that way. It feels like your feed is a reflection of your interests, and in some ways it is. But the version of your interests that it replicates is the one that kept you on the app the longest. Not the one you'd describe to someone who asks what you're interested in.

There's a difference between what you engage with and what you value. Between what keeps your attention and what you'd choose if you were being intentional. The feed is built around the first, not the second.

What you end up with is a highly personalized environment built to keep you watching rather than to serve your wellbeing, your growth, or your understanding of the world.

It looks like you. It just isn't quite you.

Why Two People See Different Worlds

Start with the same app and two different people and within days their feeds are different.

Every interaction is a signal. A like, a pause, a share, a comment, a skip, a replay. The system collects all of it and uses it to make decisions about what to show you next. Those decisions compound. A small difference in what two people engage with early on leads to bigger and bigger differences in what they're shown over time.

Eventually two people can be living in genuinely different versions of reality. Different facts. Different narratives. Different versions of what's happening in the world and what matters and who's to blame for what.

Neither of them knows it. Because from the inside your feed just looks like the world you know.

The Invisible Editor

There used to be editors.

People whose job it was to decide what information the public received. Newspaper editors. Television producers. Radio programmers. You could argue about whether they did that job well but at least they existed. At least there was a human somewhere making a choice about what information made it through and what didn't.

Now the editor is an algorithm, and it doesn't have values, judgment or a sense of civic responsibility. It has one objective. Keep people watching.

That's it. Everything else is secondary. The truth is secondary. Balance is secondary. Your mental health is secondary. What the algorithm optimizes for is time on the app, and it is extraordinarily good at that.

The invisible editor running your information stream has no interest in giving you a complete or accurate picture of the world. It has an interest in giving you a picture that keeps you scrolling.

Those two things are not the same.

What's Really Deciding What You See

The technology behind all of this is called a recommendation system.

The best way to understand what it actually does is to not think of it as a search tool and start thinking of it as a prediction machine.

It isn't finding content you asked for, it's predicting what you'll engage with before you know you want it. It's running constantly in the background, updating its model of you with every interaction, trying to stay one step ahead of your attention.

The recommendations feel like suggestions. They're closer to decisions made on your behalf by a system that knows your behavioral history better than you do.

Echo Chambers

When the algorithm figures out what you believe it tends to show you more of it.

Not because it agrees with you, but because content that confirms what you already think gets more engagement than content that challenges it. Agreement feels good. Validation feels good. Being told you're right feels good and the algorithm is very good at making you feel good in ways that keep you on the app.

The result is that over time your feed can become a closed loop. The same perspectives. The same conclusions. The same voices telling you the same things in slightly different ways, and because it's all you're seeing it starts to feel like it's all there is.

That's an echo chamber, and you didn't mean to choose it. You just kept clicking on things that felt true or interested you and the algorithm did the rest.

Filter Bubbles

The echo chamber is about what you believe. The filter bubble is about what you know.

Or more accurately what you don't know.

A filter bubble is what happens when the algorithm tailors what reaches you so completely that entire categories of reality just stop showing up. Not because anyone is censoring them, but because the system decided, based on your behavior, that you probably won't engage with them.

So you stop seeing them, and you don't know you've stopped seeing them because you don't know what you're not seeing.

This is one of the weirder effects of living inside a curated feed. The gaps are invisible. The things that got filtered out don't reveal themselves. You just gradually end up with a picture of the world with gaps in it you can't see.

Your Attention Is The Product

Everything we've been talking about exists inside a larger system.

The attention economy.

The basic idea is simple. In a world where information is infinite, attention is scarce, and scarce things are valuable. Attention then became the product that gets bought and sold, and the platforms that can capture the most of it become the most valuable companies in the world.

Your attention is the product. Your time is the inventory, and the feed is the mechanism for extracting as much of both as possible.

Advertisers don't pay for blank ad space the way they used to. They pay for *you*: your attention, packaged and auctioned in the fraction of a second before the page finishes loading. The better the machine can describe you, the more you're worth. You were never the customer. You're the inventory.

Once you understand that everything makes more sense. The scandalous content that's hard to look away from. The algorithmic rabbit holes that keep you watching for hours. The infinite scroll that has no natural stopping point. The notifications that pull you back every time you try to leave.

None of it is accidental. All of it is designed to keep you there.

Who Controls Attention?

That's a big question. Let's get into it.

A handful of companies control the feeds that most of the world looks at every day. They decide, through the design of their algorithms, what billions of people spend their attention on. What information reaches them. What emotions get activated. What they end up believing about the world.

That's an extraordinary amount of power.

It's mostly invisible. It doesn't feel like control because it's personalized. Because you feel like it's your choices. Because the feed feels like a reflection of you rather than a set of decisions being made about you.

But someone built the algorithm. Someone decided what it optimizes for. Someone chose to keep you hooked over telling you the truth, time on app over your wellbeing and growth over responsibility.

Those were choices. Made by people. In boardrooms. For financial reasons.

And those choices shape what you think about every day.

Free Will In A Curated World

There's a question that sits underneath all of this.

If what you see shapes what you think, and what you think shapes what you do, and what you see is being decided by an algorithm optimized to keep you engaged, how much of your thinking is actually yours?

That's not a comfortable question, and there isn't a clean answer.

You are not a passive recipient. You make choices. You have values and beliefs and a mind that can push back against what it's being shown. The algorithm doesn't control you. It influences you. There's a difference.

But the influence is real, and it's constant. Most of it happens below the level of conscious awareness.

So free will in a curated world isn't gone. It's just harder to carry out than we usually admit.

Who Is In Control?

Nobody, really.

That's the honest answer and it's a strange one.

There's no mastermind. No one sitting somewhere deciding what you specifically should think or feel or buy. The algorithm isn't evil. It's just optimizing for what it was told to optimize for. The people who built it weren't trying to manipulate you personally. They were trying to build something that kept people engaged and made money.

The effects are what nobody fully planned for. The echo chambers. The filter bubbles, where entire categories of reality quietly disappear from your feed without you ever knowing they were gone. The emotional manipulation. The fractured shared reality.

Nobody is driving. Not really. A set of systems is running, optimized for a set of outcomes, and the rest of us are along for the ride.

Which means the more important question isn't who's in charge.

It's whether you notice you're being driven.

How Does It Know Who I Know?

You met them once.

A party. A waiting room. A friend's cookout. You traded maybe ten words. You never got their number. You never looked them up.

Three days later, there they are. *People You May Know.*

Or it's worse than that. It's someone you went out of your way not to stay connected to. An ex. A relative you don't speak to. The app sets them at the top of your suggestions like it's doing you a favor.

That's the moment it stops feeling helpful. Not the ad that guessed your shoe size. This one. Because this one isn't about what you want. It's about who you know. Even though that's information you never told it.

So how does it know?

It's Building A Map

That suggestion was never the point. It's the tip of something much bigger.

What the app is really building is a map of your life. Who you talk to. Who you live near. Who you call when something goes wrong. Every person it correctly ties to you is another line drawn on it, Your family, your coworkers, the friend you only ever see in person, the people you'd never think to list, they are all on your map.

There's a name for it: a social graph. A model of how you connect to everyone around you. You never filled it out. You drew it by living near people, texting them, turning up in the same rooms.

The single name it hands you under *People You May Know* is the only part you're meant to see. Underneath, the map keeps filling in. The rest of this chapter is how each line gets drawn.

It's Not Your Phone. It's Everyone Else's.

Here's the part that flips the whole thing around.

You didn't have to hand over anything. Other people did it for you.

Every time someone taps *Allow* when an app asks to see their contacts, the whole address book goes up. Every name. Every number. Every email. Including yours. You are sitting in the phones of dozens of people. Your dentist, your kid's coach, the guy you sold a couch to in 2019. Any one of them granting contact access quietly tells the app you exist.

So the app builds a version of you out of scraps you never gave it. It knows your number because forty other people have it saved. It knows who you're connected to because it can see who keeps you in their pocket.

You never opened an account for it to find you. You were already easy to find. Everyone around you made sure of that.

What's Your Wi-Fi Password?

Think about the last time you heard or asked this.

You walk into someone's house, someone's office, the back room at work, and you join their network. Easy. Normal. Now your phone and their phone are sitting on the same connection, showing the same address to the rest of the internet.

Do it once, it's nothing. Do it every Sunday at the same house and a pattern forms: two devices, same network, again and again. To a system trying to map who belongs to who, that's a quiet little vote. *These two are together a lot.*

It's the same thread that lets something a roommate searched turn up on your feed. Same network, shared signal. Earlier it was your ads. Now it's the people you know.

They never explain how they do it. But the password was never really about the internet. You think you're handing over the connection. You're handing over the introduction, your phone to theirs, and neither one forgets it.

A Friend Of A Friend Of A Friend

Most of it, though, comes down to overlap.

You and a stranger share nine mutual connections. You turn up in the same group chats, tagged in the same photos, saved in the same phones. The system doesn't need to hear you say their name. It can see where your life overlaps with theirs.

If enough of your world already overlaps with someone else's, it's a safe bet you've crossed paths. Usually it's right. That's what makes it unsettling: not that it guesses, but that it guesses *well.*

All The Apps Are The Same App

And none of this stays in one place.

A new website or app lets you sign in with your Google account. You do, because it's faster. You use the same email, the same phone number, the same device for all of it. Every time, you're handing two services the same thread to tie back together.

Some of these apps are openly connected: same company, same systems behind the scenes. Others get linked through data brokers, companies whose whole business is matching who you are on one app to who you are on another. By the time they're done, your separate accounts were never really separate. They're one profile, just under different names.

Why It Lands So Hard

When it guesses an ad, it's annoying. When it guesses a person, it feels like exposure.

People have watched someone they dated once surface in their suggestions. A parent they'd cut off. In some cases, strangers who, it turned out, shared one private thing with them and nothing else. The feed reaches into the part of your life that's supposed to be yours to run and lays the whole thing on the table.

That's the real *how does it know?* It's louder here than anywhere, because it isn't about your taste. It's about who you're connected to.

Putting It To Use

It doesn't just collect all that. It uses it.

The fastest way to guess what you'll want is to find the people most like you, the ones already connected to you, and watch what made them stop scrolling.

So a video slides up and you pause. Not a like. Not a comment. Just a half-second where your thumb goes still. That pause gets recorded too and matched against everyone connected to you.

Your connections tell it who you are. The pause tells it what you'll do. Put the two together, and you stop being a stranger.

What's Really Happening

But step back and look at what actually happened.

No one listened. No one read your mind. You and everyone around you spent years feeding the same few facts, your number, your email, your contacts, your networks, your logins into systems built to connect dots for a living. The suggestion isn't witchcraft. It's arithmetic on everything that was already handed over.

Once you can see that, People You May Know stops being a mystery and turns into what it is: a handful of connections. Your number. Your email. Your contacts. Your network. Each one tied by you, or by someone standing close to you.

You can't take back the connections you've already shared. But now you can see how it works, and every time an app asks for your contacts, you can decide whether to say yes.

Why Do I Keep Picking It Up?

You're not even bored yet and your hand's already moving.

In line. At a red light. Mid-sentence in a show. The phone's in your hand before you decided to pick it up, and you couldn't say what you're looking for. You just needed to look.

That reflex didn't come from nowhere. It was built.

Somebody designed it to feel this way. The reach, the pull, the quiet sense that you're missing something if you don't check. None of it is an accident. The reason you keep reaching for it is built right into the design.

The Slot Machine In Your Pocket

Think about what happens when you pull down to refresh.

A little spin. A pause. And then, maybe something good. Maybe nothing. You don't know which, and that's the whole trick. A reward you can count on gets boring. A reward that might come, might not, never does.

It's the exact thing that keeps people sitting at slot machines. Pull, wait, maybe. Pull, wait, maybe. The feed runs on the same engine, and so does the refresh, the notification, the little red dot that means something's waiting for you.

You're not weak for chasing it. It was tuned, carefully, to be chased.

Nowhere To Stop

Why is there no ending.

A book ends. A record ends. The feed was built specifically so it never does. There's no last page to reach, no natural place where you look up and think, Okay, done. One thing autoplays into the next before you've finished the first. The design's whole job is to make sure the moment you'd have put it down never comes.

It's Not You

So when you catch yourself reaching again, give yourself a small break.

This isn't a failure of willpower. You're up against rooms full of people whose entire job was to make the device in your hand hard to set back down. They're very good at it.

Noticing the reflex doesn't make it go away. But it puts a pause between the urge and your hand, and that pause is enough to decide for yourself.

Why Was I Listening?

We've spent this whole book asking the same question.

How does it know. How does it know what I want, what I feel, what I needed to hear, where I'm headed next. Every section, a different version of it, and every answer pointed back to the same place. The system. The algorithm. The data. The prediction. The feed.

But there's a question we haven't asked yet. And it might be the more important one.

Why were you listening?

Because here's something this whole book has quietly skipped over. That tarot reading, the algorithm showed you, that it also showed to a lot of people that day. Most of them scrolled right past it. You didn't. You stopped. You watched it twice. You sent it to three people.

Same algorithm. Same content. Same moment.

The machine doesn't explain the difference.

You do.

The Door Was Already Open

Think about the last time something connected a little too perfectly.

Odds are you weren't having an ordinary day.

We've talked about how your behavior changes when your mood changes and how the algorithm reads those shifts and adjusts. But that's only half of what's happening. The other half is that when you're in a certain state, you're not just easier to read. You're easier to reach.

When you're steady, content bounces off you. A quote about letting someone go reads as a nice quote and you keep scrolling. But three weeks after a heartbreak, that same quote stops you cold. Nothing about the quote changed. You changed. You showed up that day already in a specific emotional state, already reaching for something, already looking for a sign whether you admitted it or not.

The content didn't create the need.

It walked through a door that you were holding open.

You Filled In The Blanks

This is the part many people get backwards.

You think the reading was about you. It wasn't. It couldn't have been. It was filmed for an audience of strangers by someone who has no idea you exist.

What actually happened is that the reading gave you an outline and you filled it in.

The tarot reader says someone is pulling away. They say there are feelings that haven't been spoken. They say a connection won't quite let go, and in the half second it takes to hear those words, your brain fills in the rest. Their name. The text left on read. The way things have felt off for a month. You don't notice yourself doing it. It feels like the reading knew. But the reading didn't know anything. It handed you a blank space shaped vaguely like a person, and you poured someone real into it.

That's not you being fooled.

That's you doing the most human thing there is. Taking something general and making it mean something specific. The content was the easy part. You did the hard part without even noticing.

We Wanted It To Know

And underneath all of it is something simpler, and a little harder to believe.

You wanted it to know.

Not consciously. Not in a way you'd ever say out loud. But that feeling, the one where it just gets you, feels good instead of creepy. Because being known is one of the things people want most in the world. To be seen. To be understood. To have something out there look at you and say, yeah, I get it.

We need that from each other, and when we can't get it from each other, when the people around us are busy or far away or just don't quite understand, we'll take it wherever we can find it. Even from a video made for ten million strangers. Even from a feed that can't see us at all.

That's the quiet ache underneath the whole thing. Not that the machine is watching. That we're so hungry to be seen we'll let something that can't see us pretend to.

And for a second, it works.

That second is real. That's why you stopped scrolling.

So why were you listening?

Because you were already in the middle of something. Because part of you was already reaching for something. Because you wanted, like everyone wants, for someone to understand.

The machine met you there. But it didn't start the conversation. You did. You walked up to the feed already carrying the question, already holding the feeling, already half hoping something would answer.

All this time we've been asking how it knows.

Maybe the better question was never about the machine at all.

Maybe it was about the part of us that was hoping it would.

Does It Know?

So does it know?

By now we've come at that question from several directions. We spent most of this book asking what the machine knows about you. Then, near the end, we turned it around and asked something harder. Why were you listening in the first place. Why did you stop and watch.

Think about these, because the real answer lives in the space between them.

After everything we've covered, the ads that followed you, the content that found you at exactly the right moment, the feed that seemed to understand what you were feeling before you said a word, after all of that, what's the actual answer?

It depends on what you mean by *know*.

If you mean does it have access to an enormous amount of information about you, your behavior, your patterns, your history, the people around you, and the millions of people who have behaved like you before, yes. Absolutely. More than most people realize and more than most people are comfortable with once they do realize it.

If you mean does it understand you, really understand you, the way another person can, the way you understand yourself on a good day, no. Not even close.

The gap between those two is where all of it exists.

What We Explored

We started with a feeling.

That strange, slightly unsettling experience of technology seeming to know something it shouldn't. The ad that appeared out of nowhere. The content that connected at exactly the right moment. The feed that shifted when your mood shifted. The recommendation that was delivered before you needed it.

We looked at what's actually behind those experiences. The data trails you leave just by moving through your day. The behavioral patterns that reveal more about you than you'd choose to share. The prediction models that don't need to listen to your conversations because they already know enough. The recommendation systems optimized, not for your benefit, but for your engagement. The emotional mirroring that makes your feed feel like it understands you, when really it's only learned what keeps you there.

We looked at the human side of it too. The pattern seeking brain that finds meaning everywhere it looks. The way certain feelings make us more open to certain kinds of content. The Barnum effect that makes general messages feel personal. The frequency effect that makes coincidences feel like signs. The very human need to feel seen that makes a well-timed quote feel like more than an algorithm doing its job.

All of it together is what produces the experience. Not just technology. Not just psychology. Both of them running at the same time, in the same direction.

What We Know

We know the systems are sophisticated.

More sophisticated than most people give them credit for and more sophisticated than the companies behind them will admit. The data being collected is extensive. The predictions are good. The behavioral models built around you are detailed enough to produce results that genuinely feel like something more than educated guessing.

We know the timing isn't always coincidence. A lot of what feels like the universe sending you a message is a recommendation engine that's learned your emotional patterns well enough to reach you when you're most receptive. That doesn't make the feeling less real. But it does change what's causing it.

We know the feed is not neutral. It isn't showing you the world, it's showing you a version of it, selected, shaped, and optimized by systems whose primary goal is keeping you engaged. Everything else, accuracy, balance, your wellbeing, your understanding, comes second to that.

We know you are more predictable than you'd like to be. Not completely. Not in every detail. But at a pattern level, at a behavioral level, the systems can see where you're headed before you get there. The you before you is real, and it's already in the data.

What We Don't Know

We don't know everything that's being collected.

The full picture of what data exists about you, how it's being used, who it's being shared with, and what conclusions have been drawn from it, that's not public information. We know a lot. We don't know all of it.

We don't know where the line is between prediction and influence. The algorithm learns from your behavior. But your behavior is shaped by what the algorithm shows you. At some point those two things start feeding each other in ways that are hard to untangle. How much of what you think and want actually came from you and how much of it was quietly shaped by a system that just wanted to keep you scrolling? That's genuinely hard to answer.

We don't know how good the predictions will get. What exists now is already remarkable by the standards of even ten years ago. What exists in another ten years is hard to imagine. The data will be more extensive. The models will be more refined. The gap between what the system knows about you and what you know about yourself might get narrower.

And we don't fully know what that means yet.

The Limits Of Prediction

Something worth remembering, though.

The algorithm is not you.

It's a model of you. Built from your behavior, and yeah, behavior tells you a lot about a person. But it doesn't tell you everything. It doesn't capture what you're capable of. It doesn't capture the decisions you make that break from your own patterns. It doesn't capture growth or change or the moments where you surprise yourself.

The system makes predictions based on what you've done. It has no way of knowing what you might actually do.

Predictions are built for crowds, not for any one person. Thirty percent of people like you do this. Seventy percent do that. You are somewhere in those statistics, but you are not the statistic. The pattern points toward something. It doesn't determine it.

You still get to decide.

The Limits Of Human Understanding

We're also not perfectly equipped to evaluate our own experience of all this.

Our brains find patterns. They find meaning. They remember the moments that felt significant and forget the ones that didn't. They take general messages and make them personal. They experience coincidence as intention and prediction as understanding.

None of that is a flaw. It's what makes us human. But it does mean that our intuitive sense of what technology is doing and what it knows about us is probably not entirely accurate. We overestimate it in some ways. We underestimate it in others.

The experience of being known by a machine is partly real and partly something we're constructing ourselves. The machine meets us halfway. Our minds do the rest.

The Question Remains

Even after all of this, even with a clearer picture of the data and the algorithms and the psychology and the business models behind it all, the feeling doesn't entirely go away.

You'll still see something in your feed that stops you scrolling. You'll still get an ad for something you were just thinking about. A song will still find you at exactly the right moment. A message will appear that feels like it was written for you specifically even though you now know it wasn't.

And some part of you will still wonder.

And that's okay.

Wondering is part of what makes us human. The search for meaning. The instinct to look for something more in the moments that catch us off guard. The sense that the world might be paying attention even when we know the explanation is more mundane.

The algorithm doesn't know you.

But you live in a world where something is always watching, always learning, always adjusting based on everything you do. It doesn't sleep. It doesn't forget. And it isn't holding still. Every day it's a little better at reading you than it was the day before.

You can't slow that down. Nobody can. It's bigger than any one company, any one app, any one person who built a piece of it. It just exists now, and it keeps getting better, and there's no version of the future where it suddenly knows less about you than it does today.

The line between being understood and being predicted is narrower than it's ever been and is still getting thinner. We've never been here before, and we're all still figuring out what it means.

But here's the part worth understanding. You were never going to control the machine. That was never the deal. The thing that's still yours, the only thing that was ever yours, is what you do with what it shows you.

Not the machine.

You.

Discernment

Nobody really tells you this part.

The feed was just the easiest place to see it.

Everything we've talked about in this book, the way stuff gets shaped to fit you, the way your own mind reaches out to meet it, the way something feels true just because it showed up at the right second, this doesn't only happen on your phone. It's just easier to catch there, because that's where it happens the fastest and the most often.

But It's everywhere.

It's in the news. Those headlines are built to make you feel something before you've even finished watching or reading. The people who sound so sure of themselves. The stories that just happen to line up with what you already believed. The posts, the ads, the voices that feel like they're talking right to you. All of it's after the same thing you've been reading about this whole time. Your attention.

And it all works the same way the feed does. Not just because of how it's made, but because of what you bring to it. What you're scared of. What you're hoping is true. What you already decided a long time ago.

So maybe the trick isn't figuring out how to know what's real. That might be asking too much of anybody. Maybe it's something smaller than that.

It's keeping a little space between what's true and what just feels true. Noticing when something connects because it's right, and when it connects because you were ready to hear it. Stopping for a second to ask. Who benefits if you believe it.

Not shutting your mind down, but the opposite. Keeping it open enough to poke at the stuff that feels right. Especially that stuff.

The feed was just where you practiced.

The rest is up to you.

It Knows Because You Told It

Not in words. Not intentionally. Not in any single moment you could point to and say that's when I gave it away.

But in every pause and every click and everything you watched longer than you meant to. In every search and every purchase and every time you picked up your phone because you didn't know what else to do with your hands. In every moment of loneliness or hope or heartbreak that changed the way you moved through a feed without you even noticing.

You told it everything.

And it listened in the only language it knows.

The language of behavior.

The question now isn't how does it know.

It's the one you're left with.

Maybe it knows because we tell it.

Maybe it knows because we're more predictable than we realize.

Maybe it knows because we're constantly leaving pieces of ourselves behind in the digital world.

Or maybe some experiences will always remain difficult to explain.

Either way, the next time something appears at exactly the right moment, you'll probably ask the same question again.

How does it know?

A Final Thought

If you were hoping this book would put your feelings to rest completely, I understand. I went looking for that too.

What I found instead was something more interesting. Not a clean answer, but a clearer picture. The dots connect. The picture that emerged is worth seeing, even if it leaves you with new questions instead of an answer.

We can only speculate what the whole truth might be.

If this book makes you hesitate the next time something shows up in your feed that feels a little too perfectly timed, it did its job.

A short review wherever you found this book means more than you might think. It helps other curious people find their way here.

Thank you for reading.

Brandon

www.ingramcontent.com/pod-product-compliance
Lightning Source LLC
La Vergne TN
LVHW022008200926
848481LV00007B/2289